UNDER THIS SUN

poems by

Connie Zumpf

Finishing Line Press
Georgetown, Kentucky

UNDER THIS SUN

For all my teachers.

Copyright © 2020 by Connie Zumpf
ISBN 978-1-64662-183-5 First Edition
All rights reserved under International and Pan-American Copyright Conventions. No part of this book may be reproduced in any manner whatsoever without written permission from the publisher, except in the case of brief quotations embodied in critical articles and reviews.

ACKNOWLEDGMENTS

My thanks to editors of the journals and magazines in which the following poems have appeared:

Bird's Thumb: "A Tree Falls in Texas"
Christian Century: "Emergence and Rot"
Medical Literary Messenger: "Tuesday Mermaids," "I Know You're There"
New Ohio Review: "Strangers I Think I Know"
Pilgrimage Magazine: "Three-Eyed Fox," "Morning After Yesterday"

Publisher: Leah Maines
Editor: Christen Kincaid
Cover Art: Serene René Calkins
Author Photo: Serene René Calkins
Cover Design: Daniel A. Levinson

Printed in the USA on acid-free paper.
Order online: www.finishinglinepress.com
　　　　　also available on amazon.com

Author inquiries and mail orders:
Finishing Line Press
P. O. Box 1626
Georgetown, Kentucky 40324
U. S. A.

Table of Contents

SHEDDING

Emergence and Rot 1

Strangers I Think I Know 2

I Leave Myself 4

Three-Eyed Fox 5

Tuesday Mermaids 6

Aphrodite 7

Affable Dust 8

I Know You're There 9

A Tree Falls in Texas 10

Housekeeping 11

REACHING

November Roses 15

Revival 16

Floating (Above) the Grand Canyon 17

By the Sheer Force of Song 18

Through the Bedroom Window at Georgia O'Keeffe's House 19

Morning After Yesterday 20

Last Slant of Light 22

Layers 23

Light Conversation 24

Notes 27

Additional Acknowledgements 28

*I hold a mirror to my mirror.
Suddenly, I'm a question
asking itself*

smaller and smaller

SHEDDING

I can't collect the cells I've shed.

Emergence and Rot

I see spring arrive with a pale ghost behind her.
The tulips and flax flowers didn't survive the last ax
of winter that came in May. Off with their heads!

Into the compost with brown leaves from fall,
eggshells from today; wither, decay, and maybe
next season. The year he died, my father

didn't make spring. He was gone before
crocuses came up through the snow.
This morning, his eyes and smile peered back at me

from my own silent mirror. I never know where
he'll pop up again. I see the persistence of salvia,
lavender, thyme, fed by their own past lives.

Under these buds tipped by sun, the business
of diminishment has already begun. Honeysuckle
spreads like creases and veins that twine my own skin.

Kernel to flower to seed, promise to breaking apart,
emergence to glorious rot—a rendering arc, primal
as mud on my hands—to rise up, then yield

with equal grace to the churn and suck, the dark
conditions of the clay. I strip off my gloves,
feel layers folded into the moldering muck.

I see the dead leavings of each turn and turn,
waiting for my time to turn,
down on my knees, under this sun.

Strangers I Think I Know

A woman steps off a bus or a train,
and something about her—
the way she holds her shoulders,
that straight-on walk—
swings my head around.

I am here, not over there. But maybe
there's an occasional breach
where the skin of time thins,
and I glimpse unlived versions
of myself on a crowded street,
or through bookshelves in a library.

Where do lives go
when they peel off in parallel?

I could be the ghost of a small girl
who drowned, now hovering
like an imp in her mother's thoughts.

Or a woman married, now 40 years,
a pale circle of skin under her ring,
eyes dimmed from years
of looking away.

Some might-have-been me is a doctor
who teaches psychology and practices
Tai Chi alone on the beach.

Somewhere, there's a woman
who chose the Ford
instead of the car that broke down
just south of here, the woman

who took the bus instead of the train,
who ignored the doe-eyed man
leaning against the wall.

Or is this an alternate life I'm in,
my real self's hologram
crept in under the tent flap

while embodied me pulls pints of ale
in a Dublin pub, relieved
she left Denver for a life
as an expat bartender?
She laughs at the thought
of a younger self who dreamed
of writing poetry in a parlor lined
with potted plants.

I am certain
I've stared into the hazy light
from a circus of lives I never knew,
brushed thighs with myself
on a crowded bench.

There are times even now
when my life steps out for a moment
from behind the vanishing
of what I have chosen
not to be, the parade
of what I didn't become.

I Leave Myself

I used to curse the rappity-drill
of construction down the road,
pollen coughed up in my own yard,
ashes from far-off hot disasters.
I thought they buried me in dust.

But now I know it's mostly me
shed on tables, mirrors, windowsills.

I leave myself everywhere.

Three-Eyed Fox

The three-eyed fox brushes by
as the waitress leans in,
sets down my wineglass. It curls
across her shoulder and clavicle, inked
in swirls of green and blue.
The strange sentinel stares out
from just above her breast.
She says the third eye is for her father,
the wisest man she ever knew.

Our lives converge at loss.
I've watched the etch
of my own father's life disappear,
like his ashes on the Montana plain.
Sometimes I strain to recall his face.

She is one-third my age, her art-full skin
an uncreased canvas of mistakes
not yet made. I envy her fox-guide,
its third eye an extra line of sight
set just above the dividing maze
of this life. I envy that visible mark,
the certain permanence
burned above her heart.

Tuesday Mermaids

Senior Swim

It's Tuesday, and so slow,
Van Morrison on the loudspeaker
sings us in, *la-te da.*
A graying array of urban wildebeests,
the ones the lions single out—
easy meat.

We hunker over walkers, hobble in
on canes, or stride on our own
muscle and steam on the way
to the umbrella-ringed cove, dragging
our bags of afflictions behind us.

We lower ourselves in. Suited breasts
break the surface, make wobbly ledges.

Immersion takes us like a sacrament.
Baptized sleek and young, we slip
beyond our limits. Freestyle mermaids,
lost in easy stroke beneath the glide,
now we are sylphs, the water our air,
flickering ripples edged with light.

Like lilies plucked, our grace deflates
when we emerge, gather our bones and go.
We hear the cool hum of autumn.
We know.
But today, water-diamonds beaded
to our skin, see how our August beauty
breaks the heart of summer.

Aphrodite

At first I barely notice the woman
who settles in too close

to me on the public sand.
She doesn't even glance around

as she unfolds herself
from her clothes,

exultant breasts spilling
to each side of her torso

like languid manatees lazing
belly-up on a fleshy lagoon.

Her skin is copper and sea salt.
Her laugh rolls out in waves.

Where was she when the apple
of shame was proffered?

And I must be
the anti-Aphrodite in this couplet,

fully, fiercely wrapped, shaded, draped,
a behatted mummy bundled against the sun's sizzle.

Still, I can't resist a stare
from under my floppy straw brim.

See how she sashays straight into
the foam and thrust of the ocean.

God, how she sways
with the beach's bawdy cacophony.

Affable Dust

You see them
when you stand
at just the right
angle to the light,
scrapings and flakes
we make as we collide
and rub against each other.
Our dust, like tiny moons
in slow spin,
an easy bafflement.
We can't count
how many we are
or if we are one
or whether it matters.
Sometimes we don't know
in a tangle of sleep
my limbs from yours,
or which of us is snoring.

And the mites don't care
whose past lives they eat.

I Know You're There

The signs are clear:
tiny brown pellets
along the wall
and in the cupboard
just below a hole chewed
in the cereal box.

There's a basement leak,
an attic creak, a lump
like a bullet in my breast,
a current in the air.

Clutch in the gut,
thump in the night,
and a cold blue egg
blooming
just behind my eyes.

I lock the doors,
plug the holes,
eat my kale, and walk
10,000 steps a day.

But there must be cracks
I've overlooked,
soft spots in the floor,
under my skin,
that hide these realms
of mischief just beneath
my life

where no flashlight beam
will ever reach,
and where I can see nothing
of what creeps in on silent feet.

A Tree Falls in Texas

We didn't give a thought to the possibility
    of demise
when spring called us out
       for lunch and champagne
          under a canopy
             of strapping Texas cottonwood trees.

A moment's turn, sway, snap,
     shifting flashes
of glimmer and shade. One tree cracked
    the idyll of the afternoon, fell
        in slow glide through viscous air
           like Tosca willing herself

over the parapet—we'll never know whether
    in triumph or surrender—
its splendid green death a colossal
     entanglement of limbs, branches,
        leaves, dreadlocks of its crown.
           How carefully staged, its fall

choreographed around fences, houses, cars,
    and us,
the finale over before we had time
     to imagine our afternoon's end
        as we sat, champagne in hand,
           haloed in the living sun.

Housekeeping

A bright trail of cells,
almost invisible little deaths.

I write my name in them,
then wipe them off the ledge.

REACHING

How can we help but reach
for the copper, the brass, the glinted leaf,
patches of cross-hatched light?

November Roses

The oaks out front are crackled brown,
I see their scabbly arms. We raked
bushels of acorns and leaves, said goodbye

to summer blooms, gave everything
a final pruning. And now I open
the south side gate to an encore

of roses. Scores of new blossoms
show themselves in feisty pink
against autumn's slow red and gold.

But it's too late, too cold,
it will snow tomorrow, autumn
bends away from us, there is no

stopping things. Yet here they tremble
pink in the face of coming gray, reaching,
reaching for a corner of thin November sun.

Revival

Cadillac Mountain, Maine

Today in the shadow of dawn, you and I are swept along
in a carnival of hundreds. We'll wait to be baptized
in a river of light as day splits open east of us
for the first of millions of times across our country.

We all climb the hill with baskets, blankets, babies, cameras,
drinks in covered mugs. A boy bumps a grandma along
in a wheelchair. Everyone laughs about the cold, the dark.
Polyphonies of voices. We can't see one another's faces,
can't tell who is us and other.

From the lip of Frenchman Bay we see islands like whales
wrapped in morning robes of aubergine. Everyone's draped
in blankets and down, seated on lawn chairs, on the ground,
and in backs of trucks that must have come the night before.

We wait as Earth tips toward our first view of morning.
For all the damage we have done, belching excess
into oceans and air, plundering forests, ozone, each other,
still our planet turns us so gently we can't feel it move.

Afterward, some will return to town alone, drink homesick tea
from fragile cups. Some will make love, or omelets, or both.

We'll go back to kitchens, construction sites, flickering screens,
to-do lists we'll never do, back to people we love and hate,
unforgiven sins, yet-unsprouted griefs. Some may not make it
through the week.

But this morning we stop to watch the sun's revival.
Who knows, it just might be a different light than yesterday.
Stone to stone, radiance creeps across the hill toward us.

Floating (Above) the Grand Canyon

On that Grand Canyon morning
when I went looking for God,

I stood at the rim,
expanded, then floated like hydrogen

among the ruddy temples.
I wish I could say

I soared high enough
to burn with the Fire of Truth,

but I was distracted
by the voiceless sky

dripping heat, the glint
in a raven's eye,

and a feather
that drifted like ash

taken up, then down
in slow dissolve

above the crash and spray
of an unholy cascade

light years
below.

By the Sheer Force of Song

This morning I walked at a listening slant
to the thrum of traffic, tread of my feet,
beat of my breath,

when a robin's outburst
erupted from the top of a tree.
I paused my reverie. Sometimes

you have to look up.
Such feathered swagger!
He puffed and sang,

asserted his claim
for this day's handiwork,
as though he alone summoned flowers

from huddled buds
and the sun hung in balance
by the sheer force of his song.

Something about spring
in all its brash hope,
sloughing off sparks of ambition and sass,

each tree a standing explosion
of blossoms and leaves,
each bird braggadocio a message

straight from our young, certain selves,
exhorting us to remember
every best thing we promised to be.

As though believing
in our own red-breasted invincibility
could make it so.

Through the Bedroom Window at Georgia O'Keeffe's House

> *Passing stranger! you do not know how longingly I look upon you,*
> *You must be he I was seeking, or she I was seeking...* Walt Whitman

Outside,
the guide directs us to look into her bedroom
at collections of horns and round river stones
set on ledges just the way she wanted them
turned for light and shadow.

I am the voyeur.
I impose on her ghost
padding soundlessly through the house.

I see myself
in the windowglass, superimposed
on a spare tableau: single chair, narrow bed,
white cotton spread, shallow hollow
down the middle.

I am the voyeur looking in
on seer and seen,
face-to-face, first hers, then mine.

High cheekbones, hooded eyes,
contours, lines,
mesas, arroyos, and rumble-dust roads—
a map of who I've been,
and the stranger I will yet become.

Morning After Yesterday

Feet in the air, eyes rolled back,
the dog sleeps under a tree,
tongue half-lolled as if in death.
She wakes every day
in new slobbers of joy,
head down, vacuuming the ground
for fresh astonishments of stink.
She doesn't call it a miracle, or ask
how yesterday's godsends
and grievances altered her.

And you?
What do you carry into sleep's far chambers?
What makes its way back in you,
after you blink the coins from your eyes?

You might be who you were yesterday,
were it not for the lingering smirks
of your mistakes, a new catch in your chest
from an old friend's slight,
a crack in your throat
after the bombed out storefront
flickered across your screen.

Not to mention how yesterday's sun
flamed the geraniums one by one,
or the way the moon creeps
slightly farther from Earth each day,
loosening its tug on the tides of your blood.

Now bedclothes pool at your feet,
old skin. And everything breathed in,
spat out, slapped away,
or held against your cheek
before closing your eyes still,
cell by cell,
makes its pilgrimage through you,
lighting candles,
leaving tokens along the way.
It is happening,

even this morning as you sit
on the edge of the bed
looking down at your feet,
aware of the weight of your rising
that waits
like a stone on your back
or wings.
It is happening.

Last Slant of Light

Tonight I sit in my den
and pretend to write,

idling phrases until the last
slant of light streams silent

from the room. Soon
shadows will creep into nooks,

the moon will pale this space,
my books, my pen,

as words dissolve
above a page

as clean as dreamless sleep.
I should go to bed,

but I'm caught
in that last thought

that wove its way
inside my head

just before the sun dropped.
And I know

I could stay here
warmed through the night

in the radiance of the poetry
I did not write.

Layers

Mornings I used to dress
in layers. Try on,
turn and turn
in front of the mirror,
crane my neck to see
how I was seen.
So many layers.

But none ever settled
so gently around me
as the skin of light
I'm wearing now
that tickles down
the nape of my neck,
skims every wave of rib,
drapes over
hips and thighs.

So many seasons
rippling, curving
just under it.

So many years.

Light Conversation

New-hatched turtles must totter into the night ocean
to survive. Yet, sometimes they turn away
from moonpaths on the water,
waddle inland, smitten by city skylines
clamoring with light they'll never reach.

*

        You know how it is
        to be drawn into an aura of promise
        that is not infinite, or even true. Still, I follow
        this flickering data in my palm as if
        it were angels on fire. I can't turn it off.

*

When I write alone at night, I blaze the lamps
in every room. My house becomes a nevernight.
I drink the crazy brilliance until it dribbles
down my chin, drips from fingertips,
turns my words to sweats of ink.

*

        My poems complete their turns in darkness.
        If enlightenment can be found,
        it might be there, in the muddy womb
        of ground, dense with roots,

        or through the open door of night,
        where God and I can come and go freely,
        our shadows rubbing shoulders
        as we pass each other, feeling along the walls.

*

How liquid the light that draws them in like undertow.
The eager and the innocent, the heedless and the hardy,
the ones with wings of feather and wax
who turn away from their given path
to lay themselves within the mercies of the thermals.

*

        I scrape moth skin from the patio lamp.
        Desiccated bodies, veined wings,
        tiny paper lanterns tangled in webs,
        melted onto dusty panes.

*

There is something about sunlight,
how it pulls us upward even as we burn,
how it blinds us for a moment as it sparks,
refracts from every bottle in the window
waiting to be filled.

Notes

Revival—Cadillac Mountain, Maine is the highest eastern point along the North Atlantic seaboard. In October, it is the first point at which light from the sun hits the United States.

"Looking in the Bedroom Window at Georgia O'Keefe's House"—The epigraph is taken from Walt Whitman's "To a Stranger."

Additional Acknowledgements

My gratitude to John Brehm, whose years of mentorship and critique made these poems possible.

Thanks also to Elizabeth Robinson, Andrea Hollander, and Andrea Rexilius for their teaching and guidance in shepherding these poems into a manuscript.

Special appreciation for my poetry cohort, Kirsten Morgan, Lois Levinson, Gail benEzra, Diane Alters, Erika Walker, and Harriet Stratton for their continued encouragement and wise feedback.

Thank you to my family, Paul, Callahan, Eric, Cassandra, and Jacqueline, for their love of me and support of my work.

Finally, thanks to Lighthouse Writers Workshop for providing the creative place and space in which to study and grow as a writer.

Connie Zumpf's work has appeared in *New Ohio Review, North American Review, Pilgrimage Magazine, Christian Century, I-70 Review, Human Touch, Medical Literary Messenger* and other publications. This is her first chapbook.

Connie lives and writes in Denver, Colorado. She is a longtime member of Lighthouse Writers Workshop, where she graduated from the Poetry Book Project and currently volunteers with writing outreach programs designed for people experiencing homelessness and other life challenges. She lives with her husband in what was once Lowry Air Force Base, now repurposed as an urban neighborhood. Their adult children live close by.

Educated as a developmental psychologist, Zumpf's poems often explore themes of impermanence, aging, and the human curiosity to reach into and beyond the "self we know."

www.ingramcontent.com/pod-product-compliance
Lightning Source LLC
LaVergne TN
LVHW041510070426
835507LV00012B/1455